Animals of
South America

LEVEL **2** READER

READING LEVEL
GRADES 1 TO 3

Written by Kathryn Knight
Illustrated by Edizioni Larus S.p.A.

The CREATIVE EDGE name is a trademark of Dalmatian Publishing Group,
Franklin, Tennessee 37068-2068. 1-800-815-8696.
No part of this book may be reproduced or copied in any form without written permission
from the copyright owner. CE12666/0210

Amazon Rainforest

The Amazon rainforest of South America is the largest rainforest in the world. It is home to many strange and beautiful animals. They live on the ground and up in the trees—even in the very tops of the tallest trees.

Spider Monkey

Sloth

Brocket Deer

Giant Anteater

Tapir

Hummingbird

Armadillo

Jaguar

The jaguar is the largest cat in the Americas. The dark spots are different on each jaguar. The jaguar can move quietly and skillfully through the forest. It's a good tree climber and excellent swimmer. It eats small mammals, reptiles, and eggs.

Jaguarundi

The jaguarundi belongs to the cat family, but it looks like a weasel. Like all cats, it likes to keep clean and often licks its fur.

The jaguarundi is a crafty hunter of rabbits, birds, frogs, fish, and even poisonous snakes. Rice farmers like having jaguarundis around. They eat the rats that feed on their crop.

Monkeys

The rainforest is home to many kinds of monkeys. Spider monkeys and little squirrel monkeys swing through the treetops. The big howler monkeys are the largest in the Americas. Their howls and screams can be heard as far as three miles away! Look at the thick mane of the tiny tamarin. He looks like a rock star!

Spider Monkey

Squirrel Monkey

Howler Monkey

Tamarin

Sloth

The sloth is a strange animal. It is about 2 feet long and hangs upside down from trees with its huge claws. It sleeps about 15 hours a day and moves s-l-o-w-l-y from branch to branch in search of food. It is covered with thick hair that often looks a little green because of the green *algae* (AL-jee) that grow there.

Giant Anteater

The giant anteater has a very long snout that is perfect for slipping down into termite and ant tunnels. Its claws can rip open the nest walls. Its long sticky tongue gathers lots of juicy insects. A giant anteater can eat more than 30,000 termites or ants a day!

Tapir

The tapir looks like a large pig with a trunk. It can be 6 to 8 feet long and weigh over 400 pounds. Tapirs live near water. They like to cool off by rolling in mud.

Boa Constrictor

This snake can grow to 13 feet long. It is not poisonous. It kills its prey by coiling around it and squeezing it. The boa swallows its prey whole, and then may rest for weeks to slowly digest its meal.

Poison Dart Frog

Unlike the huge boa, these tiny frogs are *very* poisonous! Their bright colors warn other animals to keep away. Native people often dip darts and arrow tips into poison taken from these frogs.

Macaw

The rainforest is filled with beautiful birds. The macaws are the largest parrots of the Americas. They come in many colors, from deep reds and greens to bright blues.

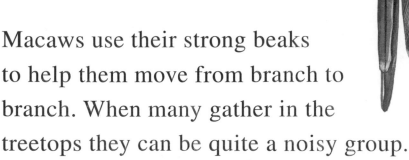

Macaws use their strong beaks to help them move from branch to branch. When many gather in the treetops they can be quite a noisy group.

Toucan

The toucan is a large bird with a very large beak. It uses this beak to reach fruit hanging on branches. Toucans are cheerful, smart birds. They gather in playful flocks on treetops in the forests.

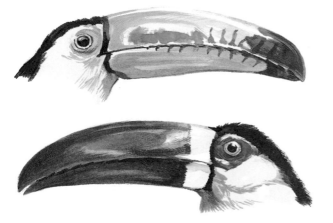

There are about 40 types of toucan, each with a different color beak.

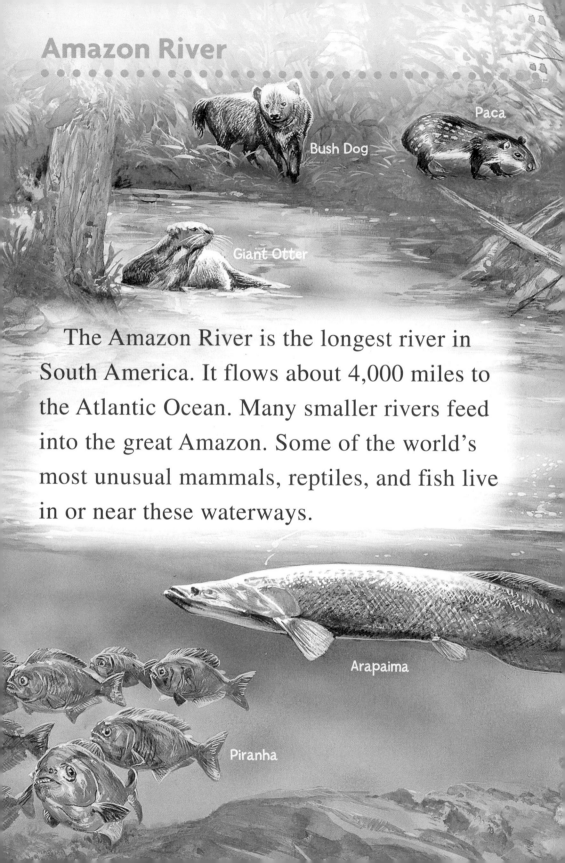

Bush Dog

Paca

Giant Otter

The Amazon River is the longest river in South America. It flows about 4,000 miles to the Atlantic Ocean. Many smaller rivers feed into the great Amazon. Some of the world's most unusual mammals, reptiles, and fish live in or near these waterways.

Arapaima

Piranha

Capybara

Anaconda

Spectacled Caiman

Basilisk

Manatee

Amazon River Dolphin

Manatee

The manatee, or sea cow, is a large, slow-moving mammal. It can be 10 to 13 feet long and weigh 1,000 pounds. It uses its flippers to move through the water and to hold onto food while it eats.

Baby manatees are about 3 feet long. They begin to eat water plants when they are only a few weeks old.

Capybara

The capybara is the world's largest *rodent* (member of the mouse and rat family). It is 3 to 4 feet long and weighs over 100 pounds! Wow! That's one big water rat! This shy animal lives near rivers and swamps. It has long, strong teeth to tear at water plants.

Spectacled Caiman

The caiman is related to alligators. It is a large reptile that can grow to 10 feet long. It has two bony crests around its eyes that make it look like it's wearing *spectacles* (eyeglasses).

Piranha

This small fish has very sharp teeth! Piranhas travel in large schools. They quickly sense when a wounded or dying animal is in the water. With their razor-sharp teeth, they rip the animal to shreds in minutes—leaving only the skeleton.

Anaconda

The anaconda is one of the largest snakes in the world. Some grow to 36 feet long. The anaconda lives alone in the swamp or on the riverbank, coiled on a low branch.

Like the boa, it is a constrictor. The anaconda grabs prey with its mouth, drags it into the water, and coils around it. Then it eats the animal whole. It can even eat a 6-foot caiman!

From the Pampas to Patagonia

In some parts of South America the land has few trees and rivers. The dry, flat plains are called the pampas. The hilly land of grass and brush is called Patagonia.

The animals that live in these areas cannot hide easily in the grass. They must be very swift or smart to escape predators. The largest predator of the grasslands is the puma. This big cat can leap more than 55 feet!

Burrowing Owl

Pampas Deer

Maned Wolf

Elegant Crested Tinamou

Weasel

Viscacha

Andes Cordillera

A long mountain chain is called a *cordillera* (cor-del-YAIR-ah). The longest chain on Earth is the Andes Cordillera. It runs 5,000 miles along the Pacific coast down to the cold southern tip of South America. In the mountains, the land is dry and the air can be quite cold.

Vicuna

Alpaca

Guanaco

Chinchilla

Most of the animals here have thick coats of soft fur. Some (llama, guanaco, vicuna, and alpaca) are related to camels of Africa and Asia. They do not need much water to live in this high, dry land.

Condor

Llama

Guanaco

The guanaco is one of the biggest wild mammals in South America. It lives in the highest areas of the Andes Cordillera. It has strong, thin legs that can run 40 miles an hour.

Llama

The llama is a *domesticated* (tamed) guanaco. It serves as a pet and pack animal. It also has fine wool used for clothing and rugs. Llamas sometimes make a humming sound. And when they are upset or nervous, they spit!

Spectacled Bear

Up in the northern mountains lives a fruit-eating bear. It has two rings around its eyes that look like spectacles. This bear is 4 to 6 feet long and can weigh 300 pounds. It is a good climber and often sleeps in the high branches.

Chinchilla

The quick little chinchilla has one of the softest coats of fur in the world. It eats moss and needs very little water. Once a male and female chinchilla form a pair, they stay together for life.